wild & beautiful

Glacier

Photography by Chuck Haney and John Reddy

FARCOUNTRY
PRESS

Right: Cow parsnip blooms on Logan Pass below Going-to-the-Sun Mountain.
JOHN REDDY

Title page: Cool and calm Lake McDonald, as seen from Apgar Village.
CHUCK HANEY

Front cover: Many Glacier Lodge glows in late-summer sunrise in this view across Swiftcurrent Lake, past Grinnell Point (at right) to Mount Gould.
JOHN REDDY

Back cover: From the Hanging Gardens at Logan Pass to the Garden Wall.
CHUCK HANEY

Endpapers: Mountain goats near Highline Trail off Logan Pass.
JOHN REDDY

ISBN 1-56037-165-X

© 2001 Farcountry Press

Photographs as marked © 2001 Chuck Haney

Photographs as marked © 2001 John Reddy

Photographs as marked © 2001 Mike Anich

Printed in Hong Kong

08 07 06 05 04   2 3 4 5

2

CHUCK HANEY

Singleshot Mountain and Lower St. Mary Lake.
CHUCK HANEY

"Wild" and "beautiful" are two words that can be heard echoing from mountain to mountain from Glacier National Park visitors. But sometimes words don't do the park justice, and superlatives are lost among towering peaks and thundering waterfalls.

The art of photography captures Glacier's timeless scenes. Sometimes there are only seconds when the light is golden on a mountain peak, or St. Mary Lake is a glassy calm reflecting the high alpine world for us mere mortals below. Photography saves fractions of time, capturing Glacier's glory to be relived over and over. This book doesn't replace being there, but I'm glad I have the chance to share those times with you.

Glacier has hooked its untamed spell on me from my very first visit. For someone raised amid cornfields, a sunrise turning mountain peaks red over Wild Goose Island on St. Mary Lake and the sight of my first grizzly bear had profound effects. What a thrill! Soon after, I was living in Whitefish, and Glacier was a nearby companion that never disappointed.

The thrill is not gone. Hikes in grizzly bear country certainly put a hop in one's step, while senses become more alert and attuned to the surroundings. When I hike with my buddy, Joe, there is always a new peak to explore as we avoid park trails and travel cross-country. Our path is the one seldom traveled and our destinations lie in a high alpine world dominated by snow-capped peaks, bighorn sheep, and every kind of weather. The Blackfeet referred to these mountains as "the backbone of the earth," and from any spiny summit along the Continental Divide, it is easy to see why.

My favorite area of Glacier is the Rocky Mountain Front, where the prairie meets the mountains. The eastern perimeter is home to verdant valleys such as Two Medicine, Cut Bank, St. Mary and Many Glacier, where the open views and abundant wildlife draw my camera most times.

I've experienced the park from many different angles and in all seasons. Spring brings the first wildflowers in the meadows, and moose calves crossing creeks with their mothers. There is freedom to explore along Going-To-The-Sun Road before summer tourists come calling.

Long summer days mean paddling a canoe across a calm mountain lake, picking sweet ripe huckleberries, or riding Going-To-The-Sun Road on my bicycle under a full moon.

Autumn splashes gold over aspen groves that accent blue skies overhead. It's the last chance to get another hike in before snow hits the high country.

Winter means cross-country skiing along a snowy McDonald Creek or soaking in the sun when it's twenty degrees below zero along the frozen shores of Lake McDonald, the sheer silence broken only by the booming crack of expanding ice.

In 2000, I hiked with my cousin, Steve, and my twelve-year-old son Logan into new country for us, along the Belly River, near the Canadian border. We sloshed along muddy trails past aspen groves budding with lime-green leaves. Then we came upon the backcountry Belly River Ranger Station. The setting was surreal. Horses grazing in an open meadow and brown earthy cabins surrounded by towering peaks. Heaven on earth, or so it seemed. On our way back, Logan mentioned he would have to take his friends on this hike when he got older. A legacy is passed to the next generation.

Chuck Haney

Swiftcurrent Creek at its beginning,
flowing out of Swiftcurrent Lake.
JOHN REDDY

JOHN REDDY

Glacier National Park…I'm not sure what else can be said in mere words. All who have seen it know what I mean. I was very small the first time I saw it, and even then it stunned me! Forty-some years later it still takes my breath away and brings tears to my eyes every time I go there. Its beauty is mesmerizing. It can be overwhelmingly majestic. And it can be soft and soothing. It can be scary and inviting at the same time. It's blindingly white and it's a rainbow of color. It roars and it whispers. How lucky we are: God blessed Glacier Park!

I dedicate my portion of this book to all the people who helped and encouraged me along the way…my friends, my teachers and my family. To my wife, Judy, who continues to push me after all these years. To my teacher John Hooten. To my teacher and mentor Rudi Dietrich, whose influence I really think is part of every good photograph I make. A special remembrance for Cal Hoiland, one of the sweetest men I've brushed by in my life…we'll meet again.

John Reddy

Above and left: East Glacier Lodge inside and out.

CHUCK HANEY

Preceding pages: Bowman Lake.

JOHN REDDY

Above: Elk herd enjoying a sunny winter day on the shore of St. Mary Lake.
CHUCK HANEY

Left: Fresh snow on the Garden Wall, as seen from McDonald Creek Valley.
JOHN REDDY

Left: Baring Creek's run through Sunrift Gorge.
CHUCK HANEY

Below: Granite Park Chalet.
CHUCK HANEY

Facing page: Morning light reaches Two Medicine Lake below Sinopah Mountain.
CHUCK HANEY

Above: Passing the Weeping Wall, one of the historic tour buses makes its way up Going-to-the-Sun Road.
CHUCK HANEY

Left: Marsh plants are a favorite bull moose snack.
CHUCK HANEY

Facing page: Rockwell Falls in the Two Medicine Valley.
CHUCK HANEY

Preceding pages: Morning breaks at Singleshot Mountain and St. Mary Lake.
CHUCK HANEY

Above: Kintla Lake, in the park's north country, once was the site for oil exploration.
JOHN REDDY

Right: Looking down to Wild Goose Island on St. Mary Lake at sunrise.
CHUCK HANEY

Above: Vegetation mosaic below Logan Pass, whose name honors the park's first superintendent, William R. Logan. JOHN REDDY

Right: Half changed into its summer camouflage, this ptarmigan is going from snow-white to pebbled brown. JOHN REDDY

Facing page: Cataract Mountain rises beyond Siyeh Creek. JOHN REDDY

Above: Morning gilds Dusty Star Mountain, named King's Mountain by a Hudson's Bay Company explorer in the 1790s.
CHUCK HANEY

Left: The North Fork of the Flathead River, below the Livingston Range, steams on a winter dawn.
CHUCK HANEY

Above: Snowflake spangles for gems of rocks.
CHUCK HANEY

Left: Clouds weave a mystic spring mood on Hidden Lake Pass.
JOHN REDDY

Preceding pages: Ready for Apgar Village guests' day
on Lake McDonald.
CHUCK HANEY

Above: By the skeletons of burned-out trees, fireweed begins
the forest's ecological cycle anew.
JOHN REDDY

Right: Cloud shadows crossing Going-to-the-Sun Mountain.
JOHN REDDY

Above: Many Glacier Lodge first served visitors who arrived by train and coach.
CHUCK HANEY

Facing page: McDonald Creek below the Garden Wall.
JOHN REDDY

Above: At Essex, just south of the park, an inviting shelter on a winter night.
JOHN REDDY

Right: Lewis' monkeyflowers sparkle pink among arnica below Clements Mountain, just southwest of Logan Pass.
CHUCK HANEY

Crisp winter day at Lake McDonald.
JOHN REDDY

Above: Grizzly bears' shoulder humps are one way of identifying them.
MIKE ANICH

Right: Cooling vision of Lunch Creek, east of Logan Pass.
JOHN REDDY

Above: Night falls on an unnamed pond near St. Mary.
JOHN REDDY

Facing page: Searching for water beside McDonald Creek.
JOHN REDDY

Above: Avalanche Creek with fresh snow.
CHUCK HANEY

Right: With pyramid-shaped Reynolds Mountain on the horizon,
forest regrowth combines with signs of a past fire.
JOHN REDDY

Above: St. Mary Lake probably was named by early "black robes" (Catholic missionaries).
JOHN REDDY

Facing page: Avalanche Creek Gorge bears icy waters even in midsummer.
JOHN REDDY

Above: Bighorn sheep finds food on a tiny ledge of Mount Wilbur in the Many Glacier area.
CHUCK HANEY

Right: Two Medicine Creek.
JOHN REDDY

Left: Historic East Glacier Train Depot.
CHUCK HANEY

Below: Jack Frost's palette paints autumn colors along Reynolds Creek.
JOHN REDDY

Facing page: A touch of autumn along Going-to-the-Sun Road.
CHUCK HANEY

Right: Up the North Fork of the Flathead River, Polebridge's only store serves as social center for scattered wilderness residents.
JOHN REDDY

Below: Lower Two Medicine Lake.
JOHN REDDY

Facing page: Red Rock Falls on Swiftcurrent Creek.
JOHN REDDY

Above: Akaiyan Falls cuts through glacial debris near Sperry Glacier.
JOHN REDDY

Left: Huckleberries attract both bears and humans to their mountain bushes.
CHUCK HANEY

Facing page: Roots of camas, seen blooming here near Cut Bank Creek, were a potato-like food for various Indian peoples.
JOHN REDDY

After the storm, on Highline Trail
at the Garden Wall.
JOHN REDDY

Above: Clearing Going-to-the-Sun Road from winter's snowfall and avalanches is a slow, dangerous job.
CHUCK HANEY

Left: McDonald Creek, swollen with early-spring snowmelt.
JOHN REDDY

Left: Grinnell Glacier.
CHUCK HANEY

Below: McDonald Creek.
JOHN REDDY

Facing page: Beargrass blooms by an icy waterfall.
JOHN REDDY

Above: Not even a high fog is likely to cause this mountain goat to make a false step.
MIKE ANICH

Left: Logan Pass Visitor Center awaits plowing out for spring.
CHUCK HANEY

Above: Lake McDonald was renamed from the Blackfeet for "Sacred Dancing Lake" to honor possibly Finian McDonald, a fur trapper around 1810, or Duncan McDonald, an area freighter in the 1890s.
JOHN REDDY

Facing page: It's night on McDonald Creek, but still day atop the Garden Wall.
JOHN REDDY

Above: Cameron Falls in Waterton Lakes National Park.
CHUCK HANEY

Right: Maskinonge Lake and Vimy Peak in Waterton.
CHUCK HANEY

Above: A cottonwood and a cedar vie for space along Trail of the Cedars.
JOHN REDDY

Left: Running Eagle Falls was named for the unusual Blackfeet woman who fasted and obtained a vision here, a rite seldom performed by women.
JOHN REDDY

Above: Looking toward Logan Pass and Logan Creek from the Highline Trail.
JOHN REDDY

Facing page: Sundown approaches Mount Oberlin and Mount Cannon.
CHUCK HANEY

Above: Hoary marmots need to munch constantly to prepare for winter.
MIKE ANICH

Left: Looking to Going-to-the-Sun Mountain
from the Hanging Gardens as night falls.
JOHN REDDY

Above: Lake McDonald Lodge.

CHUCK HANEY

Left: Fog lifts from Lake McDonald one early-autumn morning.

JOHN REDDY

Above: Two Medicine Lake

JOHN REDDY

Facing page: Below Mount Saint Nicholas, evidence of a past fire
in the drainage of the Middle Fork of the Flathead River.

JOHN REDDY

Above: An old Park Service barn sits in the lush meadow below Bad Marriage Mountain.

CHUCK HANEY

Left: Sherburne Peak and Yellow Mountain from Chief Mountain Highway, the route to Waterton Lakes National Park in Canada.

JOHN REDDY

Left: Paintbrush wearing this morning's dew.
CHUCK HANEY

Below: Fireweed in fall.
JOHN REDDY

Facing page: Glacial erratic rocks and a lone limberpine greet a new day, Chief Mountain on the horizon.
CHUCK HANEY

Above: At the Weeping Wall on Going-to-the-Sun Road, water seeps constantly through layers of limestone.
CHUCK HANEY

Left: High summer in the Saint Mary Valley.
JOHN REDDY

Above: Western larch with a birch-tree background, in autumn colors.
JOHN REDDY

Right: Prince of Wales Hotel in Waterton Lakes National Park, which adjoins Glacier in Canada.
CHUCK HANEY

Preceding pages: Beargrass (actually a lily that bears do not eat) abloom on glacier-carved Reynolds Mountain, at Logan Pass.
JOHN REDDY

Above: This whitetail buck still wears spring's "velvet,"
which nourishes his growing antlers.
CHUCK HANEY

Left: A morning storm riles Two Medicine Lake
below Sinopah Mountain.
CHUCK HANEY

Above: Spring tapestry of lupine.
JOHN REDDY

Left: Grinnell Point rise like a ship's prow over thirty-seven-feet-deep Swiftcurrent Lake.
CHUCK HANEY

Above: Going-to-the-Sun Road was dedicated in 1933.
CHUCK HANEY

Left: Bald eagles, national symbol of the United States, flourish in the park.
JOHN REDDY

Facing page: Snyder Creek in a fury among redcedar and hemlock on the park's west side.
CHUCK HANEY

Above: Lupine's purple complements paintbrush's pinks.
JOHN REDDY

Right: Swiftcurrent Lake, with Mount Wilbur in the middle distance, and the Continental Divide beyond it.
JOHN REDDY

Above: On Going-to-the-Sun Road near the Triple Arches.
CHUCK HANEY

Left: Heaven's Peak and the McDonald Creek Valley.
JOHN REDDY

Above: The brilliance of fireweed below Mount Cannon.
JOHN REDDY

Right: From Sperry Chalet, looking across McDonald Lake to Howe Ridge.
JOHN REDDY

Above: At twenty degrees below zero, ice begins to conquer McDonald Creek and Falls.
CHUCK HANEY

Facing page: Atop Marias Pass.
JOHN REDDY

Above: Stormy sunset over Mount Wilbur.
CHUCK HANEY

Left: Western larch (also called tamarack) makes a brilliant autumn accent among evergreens, then drops its needles for winter.
CHUCK HANEY

Above: Winter decorates Sunrift Gorge.
CHUCK HANEY

Right: Medicine Grizzly Peak (center) above the Cut Bank Creek Valley.
JOHN REDDY

Dusty-pastel day-opener at St. Mary Lake.
JOHN REDDY

Above: Glacial melt feeds Baring Falls.
CHUCK HANEY

Left: Looking past Boulder Peak (far left) to Hole-in-the-Wall.
JOHN REDDY

Above: Ferns fill the forest floor.
JOHN REDDY

Facing page: Hidden Lake is in a "cirque," a bowl carved by the glacier that once formed here.
JOHN REDDY

Above: Keeping breakfast safe from passing bears.
CHUCK HANEY

Right: Mount Oberlin and Mount Cannon.
JOHN REDDY

Above: Cool, crisp, and breathtaking view from Going-to-the-Sun Road to the Garden Wall.
CHUCK HANEY

Left: The Garden Wall is an "arete," remains of a mountain scraped away on both sides by glaciers.
JOHN REDDY

Above: Chief Mountain and Yellow Mountain aglow on an autumn day.
CHUCK HANEY

Facing page: Red Eagle Mountain above St. Mary Lake.
JOHN REDDY

Mount Reynolds rises in the distance beyond Going-to-the-Sun Road's east-side tunnel near Logan Pass.
JOHN REDDY

Above: Hidden Falls, in the Many Glacier area.
CHUCK HANEY

Left: Remote Belly River country in the north part of the park,
with Gable Mountain, Mount Merritt, and Bear Peak.
CHUCK HANEY

Above: Packed for the long haul, Bill
and Andy Merritt cross St. Mary Bridge.
CHUCK HANEY

Right: Trail of the Cedars boardwalk
leads to Avalanche Gorge.
CHUCK HANEY

Facing page: Haystack Creek whooshes
below the Garden Wall.
CHUCK HANEY

Fireweed flashes bright pink as the sun sets behind the Livingston Range, Glacier's west-side mountains.
JOHN REDDY